today

IS GOING TO BE A GOOD DAY

future self journal

Life is about creating yourself.
It only takes a few minutes every day to manifest
positive changes into your life.

Something wonderful happens when you put pen to
paper to set your intentions for the day. This daily
future self journal helps your mind visualise your
daily goals, so that you can breakout of your
subconscious habits, create positive changes to your
life and unlock your potentials.

ARTRA

How to use this journal

EXPLANATIONS

TODAY I AM PRACTICING   [   ]
[TO CREATE CHANGE, PICK ONE HABITUAL THOUGHT
OR FEELING TO WORK AND IMPROVE ON.]

PARTICULARLY WHEN   [   ]
[PICK A NEW BEHAVIOUR TO ALLOW CHANGE TO YOUR
HABITUAL THOUGHT OR FEELING.]

I AM GRATEFUL FOR   [   ]
[IDENTIFY WHAT ALREADY EXISTS WITH GRATITUDE.]

BY THE END OF THE DAY, I WILL FEEL [ ] BECAUSE [ ]
[IMAGINE HOW YOU WOULD FEEL BY THE END OF THE
DAY IF YOU PRACTICED THE ABOVE TODAY. LINKING A
NEW FEELING TO A NEW BEHAVIOUR WILL HELP YOU
BELIEVE IN YOUR NEW THOUGHTS.]

MY AFFIRMATION FOR TODAY
[NEW THOUGHTS AND AFFIRMATIONS CAN HELP YOU
GET OUT OF YOUR OLD HABITUAL THINKING.]

notes at the end of the day

◄ ■■■ ►

[If you have time, it is always a
good idea to reflect by the end of
the day on your progess]

How to use this journal

SAMPLE PROMPTS

TODAY I AM PRACTICING
        self love and not to criticise myself

PARTICULARLY WHEN
        I am not meeting my schedules and my inner
        self starts criticising my mistakes

I AM GRATEFUL FOR
        my ability to reflect and strive for excellence

BY THE END OF THE DAY, I WILL FEEL
        connected to myself

BECAUSE
        I was more patient and loving to myself

MY AFFIRMATION FOR TODAY
        I am enough and worthy of love

notes at the end of the day

This afternoon I made a mistake at work and I realised that I
started to criticise myself again, but my mind was reminded by
my future self journal goals which I set this morning and I
developed a secondary voice to tell myself it is okay.

" *Destiny* is not a matter of chance. It is a matter of choice. It is not a thing to be waited for, it is a thing to be achieved. "

WILLIAM JENNINGS BRYAN

Vision Board

my core values

CAREER

WELLNESS

FINANCE

RELATIONSHIPS

DATE:

TODAY I AM PRACTICING

PARTICULARLY WHEN

I AM GRATEFUL FOR

BY THE END OF THE DAY, I WILL FEEL

BECAUSE

MY AFFIRMATION FOR TODAY

notes at the end of the day

DATE:

TODAY I AM PRACTICING

PARTICULARLY WHEN

I AM GRATEFUL FOR

BY THE END OF THE DAY, I WILL FEEL

BECAUSE

MY AFFIRMATION FOR TODAY

notes at the end of the day

DATE:

TODAY I AM PRACTICING

PARTICULARLY WHEN

I AM GRATEFUL FOR

BY THE END OF THE DAY, I WILL FEEL

BECAUSE

MY AFFIRMATION FOR TODAY

notes at the end of the day

DATE:

TODAY I AM PRACTICING

PARTICULARLY WHEN

I AM GRATEFUL FOR

BY THE END OF THE DAY, I WILL FEEL

BECAUSE

MY AFFIRMATION FOR TODAY

notes at the end of the day

DATE:

TODAY I AM PRACTICING

PARTICULARLY WHEN

I AM GRATEFUL FOR

BY THE END OF THE DAY, I WILL FEEL

BECAUSE

MY AFFIRMATION FOR TODAY

notes at the end of the day
◀ ■■■ ▶

DATE:

TODAY I AM PRACTICING

PARTICULARLY WHEN

I AM GRATEFUL FOR

BY THE END OF THE DAY, I WILL FEEL

BECAUSE

MY AFFIRMATION FOR TODAY

notes at the end of the day

DATE:

TODAY I AM PRACTICING

PARTICULARLY WHEN

I AM GRATEFUL FOR

BY THE END OF THE DAY, I WILL FEEL

BECAUSE

MY AFFIRMATION FOR TODAY

notes at the end of the day
◀ ▪▪ ▶

DATE:

TODAY I AM PRACTICING

PARTICULARLY WHEN

I AM GRATEFUL FOR

BY THE END OF THE DAY, I WILL FEEL

BECAUSE

MY AFFIRMATION FOR TODAY

notes at the end of the day
◀ ■■ ▶

DATE:

TODAY I AM PRACTICING

PARTICULARLY WHEN

I AM GRATEFUL FOR

BY THE END OF THE DAY, I WILL FEEL

BECAUSE

MY AFFIRMATION FOR TODAY

notes at the end of the day

◀ ▪▪ ▶

DATE:

TODAY I AM PRACTICING

PARTICULARLY WHEN

I AM GRATEFUL FOR

BY THE END OF THE DAY, I WILL FEEL

BECAUSE

MY AFFIRMATION FOR TODAY

notes at the end of the day

DATE:

TODAY I AM PRACTICING

PARTICULARLY WHEN

I AM GRATEFUL FOR

BY THE END OF THE DAY, I WILL FEEL

BECAUSE

MY AFFIRMATION FOR TODAY

notes at the end of the day
◀ ••• ▶

DATE:

TODAY I AM PRACTICING

PARTICULARLY WHEN

I AM GRATEFUL FOR

BY THE END OF THE DAY, I WILL FEEL

BECAUSE

MY AFFIRMATION FOR TODAY

notes at the end of the day
◄ ■■

DATE:

TODAY I AM PRACTICING

PARTICULARLY WHEN

I AM GRATEFUL FOR

BY THE END OF THE DAY, I WILL FEEL

BECAUSE

MY AFFIRMATION FOR TODAY

notes at the end of the day
◀ ▪▪ ▶

DATE:

TODAY I AM PRACTICING

PARTICULARLY WHEN

I AM GRATEFUL FOR

BY THE END OF THE DAY, I WILL FEEL

BECAUSE

MY AFFIRMATION FOR TODAY

notes at the end of the day
◀ ▪▪ ▶

DATE:

TODAY I AM PRACTICING

PARTICULARLY WHEN

I AM GRATEFUL FOR

BY THE END OF THE DAY, I WILL FEEL

BECAUSE

MY AFFIRMATION FOR TODAY

notes at the end of the day

DATE:

TODAY I AM PRACTICING

PARTICULARLY WHEN

I AM GRATEFUL FOR

BY THE END OF THE DAY, I WILL FEEL

BECAUSE

MY AFFIRMATION FOR TODAY

notes at the end of the day

DATE:

TODAY I AM PRACTICING

PARTICULARLY WHEN

I AM GRATEFUL FOR

BY THE END OF THE DAY, I WILL FEEL

BECAUSE

MY AFFIRMATION FOR TODAY

notes at the end of the day

DATE:

TODAY I AM PRACTICING

PARTICULARLY WHEN

I AM GRATEFUL FOR

BY THE END OF THE DAY, I WILL FEEL

BECAUSE

MY AFFIRMATION FOR TODAY

notes at the end of the day

DATE:

TODAY I AM PRACTICING

PARTICULARLY WHEN

I AM GRATEFUL FOR

BY THE END OF THE DAY, I WILL FEEL

BECAUSE

MY AFFIRMATION FOR TODAY

notes at the end of the day

DATE:

TODAY I AM PRACTICING

PARTICULARLY WHEN

I AM GRATEFUL FOR

BY THE END OF THE DAY, I WILL FEEL

BECAUSE

MY AFFIRMATION FOR TODAY

notes at the end of the day

DATE:

TODAY I AM PRACTICING

PARTICULARLY WHEN

I AM GRATEFUL FOR

BY THE END OF THE DAY, I WILL FEEL

BECAUSE

MY AFFIRMATION FOR TODAY

notes at the end of the day
◀ ●● ▶

DATE:

TODAY I AM PRACTICING

PARTICULARLY WHEN

I AM GRATEFUL FOR

BY THE END OF THE DAY, I WILL FEEL

BECAUSE

MY AFFIRMATION FOR TODAY

notes at the end of the day

DATE:

TODAY I AM PRACTICING

PARTICULARLY WHEN

I AM GRATEFUL FOR

BY THE END OF THE DAY, I WILL FEEL

BECAUSE

MY AFFIRMATION FOR TODAY

notes at the end of the day

DATE:

TODAY I AM PRACTICING

PARTICULARLY WHEN

I AM GRATEFUL FOR

BY THE END OF THE DAY, I WILL FEEL

BECAUSE

MY AFFIRMATION FOR TODAY

notes at the end of the day

DATE:

TODAY I AM PRACTICING

PARTICULARLY WHEN

I AM GRATEFUL FOR

BY THE END OF THE DAY, I WILL FEEL

BECAUSE

MY AFFIRMATION FOR TODAY

notes at the end of the day

DATE:

TODAY I AM PRACTICING

PARTICULARLY WHEN

I AM GRATEFUL FOR

BY THE END OF THE DAY, I WILL FEEL

BECAUSE

MY AFFIRMATION FOR TODAY

notes at the end of the day

DATE:

TODAY I AM PRACTICING

PARTICULARLY WHEN

I AM GRATEFUL FOR

BY THE END OF THE DAY, I WILL FEEL

BECAUSE

MY AFFIRMATION FOR TODAY

notes at the end of the day

DATE:

TODAY I AM PRACTICING

PARTICULARLY WHEN

I AM GRATEFUL FOR

BY THE END OF THE DAY, I WILL FEEL

BECAUSE

MY AFFIRMATION FOR TODAY

notes at the end of the day

DATE:

TODAY I AM PRACTICING

PARTICULARLY WHEN

I AM GRATEFUL FOR

BY THE END OF THE DAY, I WILL FEEL

BECAUSE

MY AFFIRMATION FOR TODAY

notes at the end of the day

DATE:

TODAY I AM PRACTICING

PARTICULARLY WHEN

I AM GRATEFUL FOR

BY THE END OF THE DAY, I WILL FEEL

BECAUSE

MY AFFIRMATION FOR TODAY

notes at the end of the day
◀ ••• ▶

DATE:

TODAY I AM PRACTICING

PARTICULARLY WHEN

I AM GRATEFUL FOR

BY THE END OF THE DAY, I WILL FEEL

BECAUSE

MY AFFIRMATION FOR TODAY

notes at the end of the day

DATE:

TODAY I AM PRACTICING

PARTICULARLY WHEN

I AM GRATEFUL FOR

BY THE END OF THE DAY, I WILL FEEL

BECAUSE

MY AFFIRMATION FOR TODAY

notes at the end of the day

DATE:

TODAY I AM PRACTICING

PARTICULARLY WHEN

I AM GRATEFUL FOR

BY THE END OF THE DAY, I WILL FEEL

BECAUSE

MY AFFIRMATION FOR TODAY

notes at the end of the day

◀ ••• ▶

DATE:

TODAY I AM PRACTICING

PARTICULARLY WHEN

I AM GRATEFUL FOR

BY THE END OF THE DAY, I WILL FEEL

BECAUSE

MY AFFIRMATION FOR TODAY

notes at the end of the day

DATE:

TODAY I AM PRACTICING

PARTICULARLY WHEN

I AM GRATEFUL FOR

BY THE END OF THE DAY, I WILL FEEL

BECAUSE

MY AFFIRMATION FOR TODAY

notes at the end of the day

DATE:

TODAY I AM PRACTICING

PARTICULARLY WHEN

I AM GRATEFUL FOR

BY THE END OF THE DAY, I WILL FEEL

BECAUSE

MY AFFIRMATION FOR TODAY

notes at the end of the day
◀ ▪▪ ▶

DATE:

TODAY I AM PRACTICING

PARTICULARLY WHEN

I AM GRATEFUL FOR

BY THE END OF THE DAY, I WILL FEEL

BECAUSE

MY AFFIRMATION FOR TODAY

notes at the end of the day

◄ ••• ►

DATE:

TODAY I AM PRACTICING

PARTICULARLY WHEN

I AM GRATEFUL FOR

BY THE END OF THE DAY, I WILL FEEL

BECAUSE

MY AFFIRMATION FOR TODAY

notes at the end of the day
◄ ■■■ ►

DATE:

TODAY I AM PRACTICING

PARTICULARLY WHEN

I AM GRATEFUL FOR

BY THE END OF THE DAY, I WILL FEEL

BECAUSE

MY AFFIRMATION FOR TODAY

notes at the end of the day

DATE:

TODAY I AM PRACTICING

PARTICULARLY WHEN

I AM GRATEFUL FOR

BY THE END OF THE DAY, I WILL FEEL

BECAUSE

MY AFFIRMATION FOR TODAY

notes at the end of the day
◀ ••• ▶

DATE:

TODAY I AM PRACTICING

PARTICULARLY WHEN

I AM GRATEFUL FOR

BY THE END OF THE DAY, I WILL FEEL

BECAUSE

MY AFFIRMATION FOR TODAY

notes at the end of the day
◀ •• ▶

DATE:

TODAY I AM PRACTICING

PARTICULARLY WHEN

I AM GRATEFUL FOR

BY THE END OF THE DAY, I WILL FEEL

BECAUSE

MY AFFIRMATION FOR TODAY

notes at the end of the day

DATE:

TODAY I AM PRACTICING

PARTICULARLY WHEN

I AM GRATEFUL FOR

BY THE END OF THE DAY, I WILL FEEL

BECAUSE

MY AFFIRMATION FOR TODAY

notes at the end of the day

DATE:

TODAY I AM PRACTICING

PARTICULARLY WHEN

I AM GRATEFUL FOR

BY THE END OF THE DAY, I WILL FEEL

BECAUSE

MY AFFIRMATION FOR TODAY

notes at the end of the day
◀ ••• ▶

DATE:

TODAY I AM PRACTICING

PARTICULARLY WHEN

I AM GRATEFUL FOR

BY THE END OF THE DAY, I WILL FEEL

BECAUSE

MY AFFIRMATION FOR TODAY

notes at the end of the day

DATE:

TODAY I AM PRACTICING

PARTICULARLY WHEN

I AM GRATEFUL FOR

BY THE END OF THE DAY, I WILL FEEL

BECAUSE

MY AFFIRMATION FOR TODAY

notes at the end of the day

DATE:

TODAY I AM PRACTICING

PARTICULARLY WHEN

I AM GRATEFUL FOR

BY THE END OF THE DAY, I WILL FEEL

BECAUSE

MY AFFIRMATION FOR TODAY

notes at the end of the day
◀ ■■ ▶

DATE:

TODAY I AM PRACTICING

PARTICULARLY WHEN

I AM GRATEFUL FOR

BY THE END OF THE DAY, I WILL FEEL

BECAUSE

MY AFFIRMATION FOR TODAY

notes at the end of the day
◀ ■■■ ▶

DATE:

TODAY I AM PRACTICING

PARTICULARLY WHEN

I AM GRATEFUL FOR

BY THE END OF THE DAY, I WILL FEEL

BECAUSE

MY AFFIRMATION FOR TODAY

notes at the end of the day

DATE:

TODAY I AM PRACTICING

PARTICULARLY WHEN

I AM GRATEFUL FOR

BY THE END OF THE DAY, I WILL FEEL

BECAUSE

MY AFFIRMATION FOR TODAY

notes at the end of the day

DATE:

TODAY I AM PRACTICING

PARTICULARLY WHEN

I AM GRATEFUL FOR

BY THE END OF THE DAY, I WILL FEEL

BECAUSE

MY AFFIRMATION FOR TODAY

notes at the end of the day
◀ ▪▪▪ ▶

DATE:

TODAY I AM PRACTICING

PARTICULARLY WHEN

I AM GRATEFUL FOR

BY THE END OF THE DAY, I WILL FEEL

BECAUSE

MY AFFIRMATION FOR TODAY

notes at the end of the day

DATE:

TODAY I AM PRACTICING

PARTICULARLY WHEN

I AM GRATEFUL FOR

BY THE END OF THE DAY, I WILL FEEL

BECAUSE

MY AFFIRMATION FOR TODAY

notes at the end of the day

DATE:

TODAY I AM PRACTICING

PARTICULARLY WHEN

I AM GRATEFUL FOR

BY THE END OF THE DAY, I WILL FEEL

BECAUSE

MY AFFIRMATION FOR TODAY

notes at the end of the day

DATE:

TODAY I AM PRACTICING

PARTICULARLY WHEN

I AM GRATEFUL FOR

BY THE END OF THE DAY, I WILL FEEL

BECAUSE

MY AFFIRMATION FOR TODAY

notes at the end of the day

DATE:

TODAY I AM PRACTICING

PARTICULARLY WHEN

I AM GRATEFUL FOR

BY THE END OF THE DAY, I WILL FEEL

BECAUSE

MY AFFIRMATION FOR TODAY

notes at the end of the day

DATE:

TODAY I AM PRACTICING

PARTICULARLY WHEN

I AM GRATEFUL FOR

BY THE END OF THE DAY, I WILL FEEL

BECAUSE

MY AFFIRMATION FOR TODAY

notes at the end of the day
◀ ■■ ▶

DATE:

TODAY I AM PRACTICING

PARTICULARLY WHEN

I AM GRATEFUL FOR

BY THE END OF THE DAY, I WILL FEEL

BECAUSE

MY AFFIRMATION FOR TODAY

notes at the end of the day

DATE:

TODAY I AM PRACTICING

PARTICULARLY WHEN

I AM GRATEFUL FOR

BY THE END OF THE DAY, I WILL FEEL

BECAUSE

MY AFFIRMATION FOR TODAY

notes at the end of the day

DATE:

TODAY I AM PRACTICING

PARTICULARLY WHEN

I AM GRATEFUL FOR

BY THE END OF THE DAY, I WILL FEEL

BECAUSE

MY AFFIRMATION FOR TODAY

notes at the end of the day

DATE:

TODAY I AM PRACTICING

PARTICULARLY WHEN

I AM GRATEFUL FOR

BY THE END OF THE DAY, I WILL FEEL

BECAUSE

MY AFFIRMATION FOR TODAY

notes at the end of the day

DATE:

TODAY I AM PRACTICING

PARTICULARLY WHEN

I AM GRATEFUL FOR

BY THE END OF THE DAY, I WILL FEEL

BECAUSE

MY AFFIRMATION FOR TODAY

notes at the end of the day

DATE:

TODAY I AM PRACTICING

PARTICULARLY WHEN

I AM GRATEFUL FOR

BY THE END OF THE DAY, I WILL FEEL

BECAUSE

MY AFFIRMATION FOR TODAY

notes at the end of the day
◄ ••• ►

DATE:

TODAY I AM PRACTICING

PARTICULARLY WHEN

I AM GRATEFUL FOR

BY THE END OF THE DAY, I WILL FEEL

BECAUSE

MY AFFIRMATION FOR TODAY

notes at the end of the day

DATE:

TODAY I AM PRACTICING

PARTICULARLY WHEN

I AM GRATEFUL FOR

BY THE END OF THE DAY, I WILL FEEL

BECAUSE

MY AFFIRMATION FOR TODAY

notes at the end of the day

DATE:

TODAY I AM PRACTICING

PARTICULARLY WHEN

I AM GRATEFUL FOR

BY THE END OF THE DAY, I WILL FEEL

BECAUSE

MY AFFIRMATION FOR TODAY

notes at the end of the day
◄••►

DATE:

TODAY I AM PRACTICING

PARTICULARLY WHEN

I AM GRATEFUL FOR

BY THE END OF THE DAY, I WILL FEEL

BECAUSE

MY AFFIRMATION FOR TODAY

notes at the end of the day

DATE:

TODAY I AM PRACTICING

PARTICULARLY WHEN

I AM GRATEFUL FOR

BY THE END OF THE DAY, I WILL FEEL

BECAUSE

MY AFFIRMATION FOR TODAY

notes at the end of the day
◄ ■■

DATE:

TODAY I AM PRACTICING

PARTICULARLY WHEN

I AM GRATEFUL FOR

BY THE END OF THE DAY, I WILL FEEL

BECAUSE

MY AFFIRMATION FOR TODAY

notes at the end of the day

◀ ••• ▶

DATE:

TODAY I AM PRACTICING

PARTICULARLY WHEN

I AM GRATEFUL FOR

BY THE END OF THE DAY, I WILL FEEL

BECAUSE

MY AFFIRMATION FOR TODAY

notes at the end of the day
◀ •• ▶

DATE:

TODAY I AM PRACTICING

PARTICULARLY WHEN

I AM GRATEFUL FOR

BY THE END OF THE DAY, I WILL FEEL

BECAUSE

MY AFFIRMATION FOR TODAY

notes at the end of the day

DATE:

TODAY I AM PRACTICING

PARTICULARLY WHEN

I AM GRATEFUL FOR

BY THE END OF THE DAY, I WILL FEEL

BECAUSE

MY AFFIRMATION FOR TODAY

notes at the end of the day
◀ ■■■ ▶

DATE:

TODAY I AM PRACTICING

PARTICULARLY WHEN

I AM GRATEFUL FOR

BY THE END OF THE DAY, I WILL FEEL

BECAUSE

MY AFFIRMATION FOR TODAY

notes at the end of the day

DATE:

TODAY I AM PRACTICING

PARTICULARLY WHEN

I AM GRATEFUL FOR

BY THE END OF THE DAY, I WILL FEEL

BECAUSE

MY AFFIRMATION FOR TODAY

notes at the end of the day
◀ ●● ▶

DATE:

TODAY I AM PRACTICING

PARTICULARLY WHEN

I AM GRATEFUL FOR

BY THE END OF THE DAY, I WILL FEEL

BECAUSE

MY AFFIRMATION FOR TODAY

notes at the end of the day

DATE:

TODAY I AM PRACTICING

PARTICULARLY WHEN

I AM GRATEFUL FOR

BY THE END OF THE DAY, I WILL FEEL

BECAUSE

MY AFFIRMATION FOR TODAY

notes at the end of the day

DATE:

TODAY I AM PRACTICING

PARTICULARLY WHEN

I AM GRATEFUL FOR

BY THE END OF THE DAY, I WILL FEEL

BECAUSE

MY AFFIRMATION FOR TODAY

notes at the end of the day
◀ ••• ▶

DATE:

TODAY I AM PRACTICING

PARTICULARLY WHEN

I AM GRATEFUL FOR

BY THE END OF THE DAY, I WILL FEEL

BECAUSE

MY AFFIRMATION FOR TODAY

notes at the end of the day

DATE:

TODAY I AM PRACTICING

PARTICULARLY WHEN

I AM GRATEFUL FOR

BY THE END OF THE DAY, I WILL FEEL

BECAUSE

MY AFFIRMATION FOR TODAY

notes at the end of the day

DATE:

TODAY I AM PRACTICING

PARTICULARLY WHEN

I AM GRATEFUL FOR

BY THE END OF THE DAY, I WILL FEEL

BECAUSE

MY AFFIRMATION FOR TODAY

notes at the end of the day
◀ ▪▪

DATE:

TODAY I AM PRACTICING

PARTICULARLY WHEN

I AM GRATEFUL FOR

BY THE END OF THE DAY, I WILL FEEL

BECAUSE

MY AFFIRMATION FOR TODAY

notes at the end of the day

◀ •• ▶

DATE:

TODAY I AM PRACTICING

PARTICULARLY WHEN

I AM GRATEFUL FOR

BY THE END OF THE DAY, I WILL FEEL

BECAUSE

MY AFFIRMATION FOR TODAY

notes at the end of the day
◀ ••• ▶

DATE:

TODAY I AM PRACTICING

PARTICULARLY WHEN

I AM GRATEFUL FOR

BY THE END OF THE DAY, I WILL FEEL

BECAUSE

MY AFFIRMATION FOR TODAY

notes at the end of the day

DATE:

TODAY I AM PRACTICING

PARTICULARLY WHEN

I AM GRATEFUL FOR

BY THE END OF THE DAY, I WILL FEEL

BECAUSE

MY AFFIRMATION FOR TODAY

notes at the end of the day

DATE:

TODAY I AM PRACTICING

PARTICULARLY WHEN

I AM GRATEFUL FOR

BY THE END OF THE DAY, I WILL FEEL

BECAUSE

MY AFFIRMATION FOR TODAY

notes at the end of the day

DATE:

TODAY I AM PRACTICING

PARTICULARLY WHEN

I AM GRATEFUL FOR

BY THE END OF THE DAY, I WILL FEEL

BECAUSE

MY AFFIRMATION FOR TODAY

notes at the end of the day

DATE:

TODAY I AM PRACTICING

PARTICULARLY WHEN

I AM GRATEFUL FOR

BY THE END OF THE DAY, I WILL FEEL

BECAUSE

MY AFFIRMATION FOR TODAY

notes at the end of the day

DATE:

TODAY I AM PRACTICING

PARTICULARLY WHEN

I AM GRATEFUL FOR

BY THE END OF THE DAY, I WILL FEEL

BECAUSE

MY AFFIRMATION FOR TODAY

notes at the end of the day

DATE:

TODAY I AM PRACTICING

PARTICULARLY WHEN

I AM GRATEFUL FOR

BY THE END OF THE DAY, I WILL FEEL

BECAUSE

MY AFFIRMATION FOR TODAY

notes at the end of the day

DATE:

TODAY I AM PRACTICING

PARTICULARLY WHEN

I AM GRATEFUL FOR

BY THE END OF THE DAY, I WILL FEEL

BECAUSE

MY AFFIRMATION FOR TODAY

notes at the end of the day

Printed in Great Britain
by Amazon